How Chinese Immigrants Made America Home

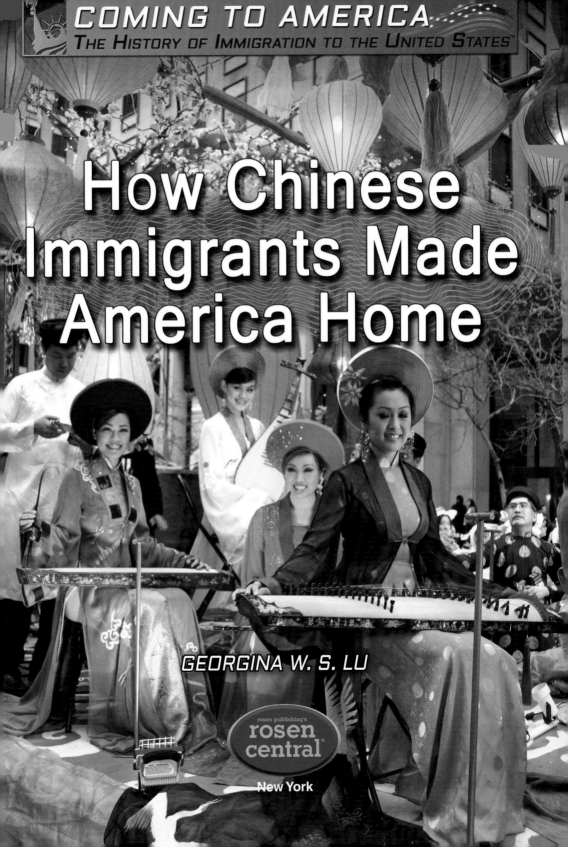

How Chinese Immigrants Made America Home

GEORGINA W. S. LU

rosen publishing's
rosen central

New York

To those who have to live with a red squiggly line under their names in Microsoft Word

Published in 2019 by The Rosen Publishing Group, Inc.
29 East 21st Street, New York, NY 10010

First Edition

Library of Congress Cataloging-in-Publication Data

Names: Lu, Georgina W. S., author.
Title: How Chinese immigrants made America home / Georgina WS Lu.
Description: New York : Rosen Central, 2019. | Series: Coming to America: the history of immigration to the United States | Includes bibliographical references and index. | Audience: Grades 5–8.
Identifiers: LCCN 2017044274 | ISBN 9781508181170 (library bound) | ISBN 9781508181187 (pbk.)
Subjects: LCSH: Chinese—United States—History—Juvenile literature. | Chinese Americans—History—Juvenile literature. | Immigrants—United States—History—Juvenile literature. | China—Emigration and immigration—History—Juvenile literature. | United States—Emigration and immigration—History—Juvenile literature.
Classification: LCC E184.C5 L76 2019 | DDC 973/.04951—dc23
LC record available at https://lccn.loc.gov/2017044274

Manufactured in the United States of America

On the cover: Celebrations of Chinese New Year are one way for Chinese immigrants to the United States to connect with their heritage.

CONTENTS

Newly arrived immigrants from China—mostly male laborers—are checking and claiming their luggage outside the immigration station on Angel Island in California.

VISA UNITED STATE
OF AMERIC

Throughout history, mass migration has largely been motivated by the need to escape danger and to seek a better life. The Chinese diaspora in the United States of America is no exception. In the mid-nineteenth century, external threats to China were looming large, and internal crises were brewing. Britain won the Opium Wars in 1842 and 1860, leaving the Manchu-led Qing dynasty in China no choice but to sign a series of unfavorable treaties with European states. The defeat also left parts of China in a semicolonial state.

Internally, civil wars were soon to start as rebel groups in the south planned to topple the corrupt Qing dynasty. This conflict eventually led to political unrest across the country. To make matters worse, famine ravaged China, and food production could not keep up with population growth. For many people, emigration was their best bet.

Initially, Southeast Asia was the most popular destination because it was close to home. However, when the news about the gold hills in California spread to China, more and more people decided to brave the rough seas and sail to America. These men hoped that they could bring their newfound wealth back home and secure a better future for their families.

Little did these men know that they would face unfair legal barriers and suffer racial discrimination in the New World. They would find that crossing the Pacific was the easy part, and that assimilating into American society was the real challenge. In the early days, most Chinese immigrants were perceived as outsiders who had no place in America. They were meant to go home once their employment contracts expired. In fact, for nearly sixty years, Chinese immigrants were excluded from entry by law. Unfazed by mainstream society's prejudice against them, some of these immigrants stayed to become a part of American society.

For early Chinese immigrants, assimilation was second to survival. They fought for better wages, banded together where they were accepted, and tried their best to pick up American customs and habits when they weren't struggling for the basics of their survival. Their descendants continued to take on the project of Americanization and contribute to American life in myriad ways.

Chinese immigrants found that assimilation is inadvertently a two-way process. As they gave up some of their old customs in an attempt to fit in, they also brought new elements to the cultural mosaic in America. By the early twentieth century, immigration restrictions had been lifted. Chinese Americans and Chinese immigrants were able to thrive in different sectors of American society after World War II up to today. In the modern era, they found much less holding them back than ever before. What follows tells their stories.

Eyeing Opportunities Across the Pacific

C hina had recognized the American continents on its world map as early as the fifteenth century. However, Chinese people did not migrate to the United States until 1848, during a particularly tumultuous time in China under the Manchu emperors of the Qing dynasty. The First Opium War, a conflict between the Qing dynasty and the United Kingdom that lasted from 1839 to 1842, had just ended six years earlier. China's loss brought economic hardship and international humiliation, as reconciliation

VISA UNITED STAT

required the Qing dynasty to sign a treaty that greatly favored the United Kingdom.

Then, domestic problems began to emerge. Revolutions against the Manchu government wreaked havoc. Political instability aggravated economic woes. To make things worse, famine suddenly struck southern China, leaving many people desperate. Frustrated with the difficulties of life at home, some decided to seek economic opportunities overseas.

LEAVING CHINA

The first Chinese immigrants—two men and a woman—arrived in San Francisco in 1848. They were soon joined by the rest of the first wave of Chinese immigrants, a group from Taishan, a city in the province of Canton, and other parts of the Pearl River delta. These first Chinese immigrants mostly spoke the Chinese dialects Taishanese and Cantonese.

The Taiping Rebellion, an anti-Manchu movement, broke out in 1850. It quickly turned into a civil war and caused the first wave of Chinese immigration. Warriors pillaged towns and villages and killed an estimated twenty million to thirty million people as the millenarian Christians often referred to as Taipings attempted to usurp power from the ruling Qing dynasty. Fearing loss of life and livelihood, many fled their homes and moved overseas.

The number of Chinese immigrants in the United States increased exponentially during and after the Taiping Rebellion. According to historian Erika Lee, in 1849, emigration from

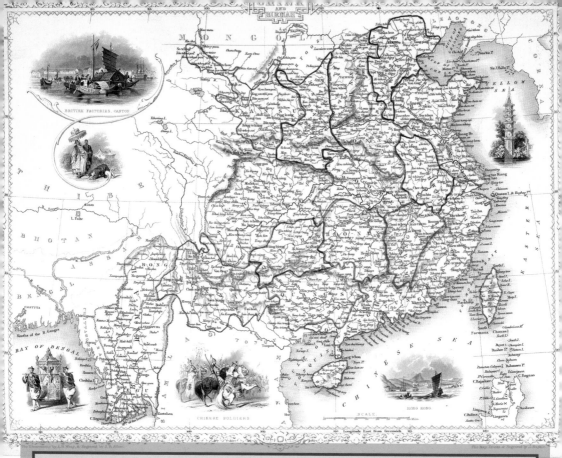

This is an 1851 map of China, then under the rule of the Manchus. Most Chinese immigrants in the nineteenth and twentieth centuries were from the Southern provinces of Guangdong and Fujian.

China to the United States was almost nonexistent. Around three thousand Chinese people had arrived in the United States by 1852, and that number would be at least five times greater by the late 1850s. By 1870, there were around sixty thousand immigrants who had come from China.

Early Chinese immigrants had a distinct profile. Many male laborers who faced unstable conditions in their home-towns decided to leave China. Married women were advised against following their husbands overseas. In the nineteenth century, Chinese society believed that a woman's place was at home taking care of her children and her husband's extended family. Because of these expectations, the majority of Chinese immigrants in the nineteenth century were men.

Leaving China was a brutal journey—one was lucky to survive and make it to American shores. While wealthy Chinese businessmen traveled in the first class sections of the ships, laborers—the majority of Chinese immigrants—were packed into the lower decks. Each laborer was given only a flat box to sleep in. The conditions on the ships were wholly inadequate. A large number of lower-class travelers died during the voyage.

JOINING THE CALIFORNIA GOLD RUSH

While a handful of people went to the East Coast, most Chinese immigrants in the mid-nineteenth century came to California because of the gold rush in 1849. The fact that they went to California in that year with the rest of the gold rush crowd made them part of the so-called forty-niners. In fact, the first generation of Chinese immigrants was called *gam san haak*, which means "gold hill visitors" in Cantonese.

At this time, immigrants from China started to arrive in groups. These immigrants—still mostly men—longed to bring home a literal pot of gold. However, reality presented them with a starkly different picture. California recruiters used the credit-ticket system to hire workers: they paid for workers' food and travel expenses in advance, and workers

THE FIRST CHINESE AMERICAN CIVIL RIGHTS ACTIVIST

Wong Chin Foo (1847–1898) was one of the most vocal fighters for civil rights for the Chinese. He was brought to American soil when he was twenty years old and was naturalized at twenty-seven. A preacher by training and a lecturer by profession, Wong wrote essays and delivered speeches to dispel the misconception that Chinese people were less civilized or moral than white people. In a bid to debunk anti-Chinese myths, he offered five hundred dollars to anyone who could prove the rumor that Chinese people ate rats.

Wong was also the voice for Chinese immigrants who wished to become

This portrait shows Wong Chin Foo in his traditional Qing-style suit and robe. Like most men in the Qing Dynasty, Wong also ties his hair in a queue.

VISA UNITED STATES OF AMERIC

American citizens. Wong made efforts to convince his compatriots in the States to change their hairstyles and attire and adopt American customs. He also tried to set up a Chinese publication called *Chinese American.* This publication was a commercial failure, but it successfully popularized the concept of an ethnically Chinese American citizen. The idea of the Chinese American was rather new to first-generation immigrants. Thus, although Wong did not create Chinese Americans, with his help, the concept of a Chinese American identity became more accepted.

were expected to pay their debt by working on a long-term basis. To make newcomers' financial situation worse, state authorities also subjected Chinese miners to unfair taxation. In 1850, California levied a twenty dollars per month Foreign Miners Tax on every non-American miner.

Notwithstanding the unfair terms, the number of contract workers from China kept rising. Their prospects in California still seemed much brighter than at home, where political upheavals were sweeping the country. Also, Californian recruiters successfully used false advertising to attract those who were eager to leave their impoverished, war-torn hometowns. Recruiters purposefully left out details about the harsh working conditions and unfair terms and exaggerated the riches of America. As read one advertisement, "Americans are very rich people … Money is in great plenty and to spare in America." The trap was sprung.

WORKING ON THE TRANSCONTINENTAL RAILROAD

By the 1860s, the California gold rush had slowed down. Chinese laborers started to work on railroads because the demand for railroad workers became high. The first railroad company to hire Chinese workers was the Central Pacific Railroad.

Not only were Chinese workers underpaid, they were also overworked. But that wasn't all. In 1862, California's government mandated that every Chinese person age eighteen and over pay $2.50 per month for a police tax. With salaries as low as $30 per month, this tax was a substantial burden. The work of Chinese laborers was also often especially dangerous. Chinese workers were frequently assigned tasks like working with dynamite.

One would expect that immigrant workers, who suffered so much for the railroad, would receive commendations and recognition from their employers. However, the work of Chinese immigrants was not acknowledged in the nineteenth century. Though Chinese migrant workers made up two-thirds of the workforce of the railroad companies, by the railroad's com-

A group of workers from China are laying railroad tracks for the transcontinental railroad. They are immigrants who came from the ships in the background.

pletion on May 10, 1869, according to the Central Pacific Railroad Photographic History Museum, they are absent in official records and photos. They were made to be invisible.

These are but a few of the humiliations and disproportionate burdens of Chinese immigrants who worked on railroads.

NO CHOICE BUT TO STAY IN CHINATOWN

Many Chinese men anticipated working in the agricultural sector. According to the Center for Labor Education & Research at the University of Hawai'i, West O'ahu, there were approx-

NOT JUST LABORERS: NINETEENTH-CENTURY CHINESE SCHOLARS IN AMERICA

In 1872, the Qing government in China decided to send thirty male students to America on a scholarship. These students were part of a program called the Chinese Educational Mission. This initiative was driven by the emperor's realization that technological and economic progress in China was behind that of the West. Thus, students in the program were expected to take classes in engineering and science at top universities so that they could contribute to the development back in China. Between the program's inception in 1872 and the Qing dynasty government shutting it down in 1881, China sent more than one hundred students to the United States.

imately forty-six thousand Chinese laborers who migrated to Hawaii to work on sugar plantations between 1850 and 1900. The community grew so fast and large that they even set up their own Chinese-language newspaper.

In Hawaii and many other states, as more and more men found work and settled in America, some of their wives and children followed. They formed Chinese communities in ethnic enclaves in what were called gateway cities. These gateway cities were major cities, such as San Francisco and New York City. They concentrated their population in parts of these cities. According to a 1997 documentary broadcast on PBS, those areas of concentrated Chinese populations came to be known as Chinatowns in 1853. Founded in 1848, the Chinatown in San Francisco is the oldest of its kind. The oldest Chinatown on the East Coast is the one in Lower Manhattan. That neighborhood was founded in the 1870s.

A common misconception is that Chinatowns were a form of self-imposed segregation or a refusal to blend in with mainstream society. However, in reality, Chinese immigrants were forced to stay in Chinatown because of racial discrimination. During the nineteenth century, the Chinese could not afford to own property outside of Chinatown. Additionally, children of Chinese immigrants were not allowed to attend most white schools.

In their beginnings, Chinatowns were very isolated from mainstream society. Part of the isolation of a Chinatown was its apparent foreignness, but some part was because it was also associated with prostitution, gambling, and gang-related activities. Nonetheless, Chinatown was an ideal landing place for working-class immigrants. For first-generation immigrants who spoke little to no English, Chinatown was where they could work, shop, and socialize with ease. It was, and still is, where traditions from different parts of China are interwoven.

Pagodas were built, dim sum restaurants were set up, Chinese schools were founded, lion dance troupes were formed. Chinatown is where immigrants celebrate the Lunar New Year—a major Chinese holiday—with great pomp. Moreover, Chinatown preserves many customs that were tamped down in China during the Cultural Revolution—for instance, the worship of Mazu. To some extent, the American Chinatown is a time capsule in which traditions and cultures are kept alive.

A Chinese American public school teacher taught newly arrived immigrant children how to write their names in English and in Chinese.

The various Chinatowns also became places where Chinese and American cultures met and mingled. For instance, Chinese chefs had to make adjustments to their recipes because some of the traditional ingredients and seasonings were unavailable in the United States. They also needed to adapt existing cuisines or invent new dishes to cater to American customers. For example, General Tso's chicken is a staple of Chinese restaurants in the United States, but it is virtually unheard of in China. Chinese food in America is an instance of two seemingly radically different cultures finding ways to fuse together and create bicultural products.

CHAPTER TWO

Brewing Resentment

D uring the 1860s, railroad and other company owners were eager to capitalize on the labor of Chinese immigrant workers because they were cheap and industrious. However, many white workers and unions viewed the influx of Chinese immigrants in the early nineteenth century as a form of economic and cultural invasion. The dominant fear was that Chinese workers were taking jobs that white people might have otherwise been hired to do. In time, those fears would result in violence and destruction.

HATRED RISES

When the economy slumped in the 1870s, widespread unemployment and fierce competition for jobs caused the fear of immigrants to intensify. Jobless men wanted someone to blame for their dismissal, and immigrant workers were easy targets.

Several politicians decided to participate in vilifying Chinese immigrants. Most notably, Samuel Gompers, a labor union leader, pitted American-born workers against Chinese laborers using the analogy "meat v. rice." The idea of rice replacing meat gave the false impression that Chinese immigrants were eroding American values in some fundamental way. Campaigns based on fear mongering, though lacking any factual basis, quickly gained support from white supremacists in the United States.

Discrimination against Chinese immigrants was mainly based on the misconception that Asians are an inferior race and that they are less human than white people. As an example of racism against Chinese people look at the words of Horace Greeley, founder of the *New-York Tribune*, to demonstrate the prevailing attitude toward the Chinese. Greeley claimed that "the Chinese are uncivilized, unclean, and filthy beyond all conception without any of the higher domestic or social relations." Those who were biased against the Chinese also saw them as carriers of so-called "Oriental diseases," such as hookworm and liver fluke. Albeit irrational, this xenophobia resonated with the public.

Samuel Gompers was originally from England. After he became a naturalized citizen of the United States, he became a labor leader who protested against foreign laborers in the name of protecting white American workers.

VISA UNITED STATES OF AMERICA

ANTI-CHINESE RIOTS ACROSS THE COUNTRY

Hostility against Chinese immigrants was common from the start, but there hadn't yet been large-scale riots. At least there hadn't been until after the death of Robert Thompson, a Los Angeles saloon owner who was mistakenly killed during a fight between two rival Chinese gangs.

Instead of going after the killer, the five hundred rioters tried to capture innocent Chinese men and boys. Those who did not manage to flee the scene in time were caught and then shot or hanged. On that chilly October night in 1871, seventeen Chinese immigrants—men and boys—were killed by a mob in Los Angeles.

The California Supreme Court initially convicted eight men of manslaughter, but the ruling was overturned shortly after. Some believed that the prosecutor tried to downplay the severity of the incident. In the aftermath, the killing, coupled with the court's indifference to the anti-Chinese violence, sent a clear message to Chinese immigrants.

After the Los Angeles massacre, anti-Chinese riots surged in California. The expulsion of Chinese immigrants in Eureka, California, in 1885 happened after an incident that mirrored almost exactly what had happened in Los Angeles. A councilman and a boy were accidentally killed in a Chinese gang fight, and white people in the community retaliated. About three hundred Chinese residents were ordered to leave Eureka immediately. Innocent men and women who were not involved in gang activities were also banished because the town council wanted Eureka to be free of Chinese influence.

Anti-Chinese movements also gained traction outside California. In September 1885, racial tension between white and Chinese coal miners in Rock Springs, Wyoming, came to a head. Some white miners held a grudge against Chinese laborers, who were paid a lower wage and were therefore more likely to get hired. Thus, a band of white workers decided to terrorize Chinese miners by assaulting them and setting their homes on fire. Hundreds of Chinese miners were driven out of

This hand-colored woodcut depicts the chaotic scene of Chinese workers fleeing white attackers in Rock Springs, Wyoming, during a riot. They are carrying all of their belongings.

town as their homes in Chinatown were burned to the ground. Local authorities did little to intervene, and no individual was held accountable for the rampage. Contradictory accounts in the press also muddied the truth of what sparked the riot. Regardless, twenty-eight Chinese workers were killed. This incident is now known as the Rock Springs Massacre.

In all of the anti-Chinese demonstrations and riots, innocent people, rather than culpable parties, were harmed.

OFFICIALLY EXCLUDED

The law and public opinion have historically informed each other in the United States. Therefore, it is hard to tell if anti-Chinese sentiment drove legislative change or if anti-Chinese laws fueled xenophobia.

What is clear is that immigration restrictions were put in place around the same time as riots against Chinese immigrants. Lawmakers voted to restrict working-class Chinese laborers from entering the country. In 1882, President Chester A. Arthur signed the Chinese Exclusion Act to impose a total ban on Chinese laborers.

Contrary to popular belief, the Chinese Exclusion Act did not ban all Chinese people from entering the United States; it targeted only working-class Chinese. Under the provisions, travelers were required to declare their professions. Diplomats, merchants, students, and their dependents were granted entry, while laborers were asked to return to China.

Despite the new law, some working-class laborers tried to enter by creating false documents to fool officials into

FEAR OF CHINESE IMMIGRANTS FOUND IN ART

The demonization of Chinese immigrants became a popular trope in artwork, cartoons, and advertisements. One example is a drawing titled *The American Gulliver and Chinese Lilliputians*, which was included in the 1902 book *Some Reasons for Chinese Exclusion. Meat vs. Rice. American Manhood Against Asiatic Coolieism. Which Shall Survive?* The artist references Jonathan Swift's book *Gulliver's Travels* and compares Chinese immigrants to the small and small-minded Lilliputians who try to take advantage of the giant that is America. This drawing characterizes Chinese immigrants as cunning creatures who wish to take over America. It belies the fact that most immigrants in the nineteenth century were honest workers who simply wanted to earn more money to support their families back home.

Similarly, artist George Frederick Keller drew a cartoon depicting a stereotypical Chinese laborer—who wore the queue, a braid worn at the back of the head, and tattered clothes—standing in the place of the Statue of Liberty in New York Harbor. The Chinese statue's foot rests on a skull, which presumably symbolizes the death of white men's livelihood. Behind the statue is a city full of dirty streets, which insinuates that Chinese immigrants brought filth to America. This incendiary drawing made it to the cover of a satire magazine called *The Wasp* in 1881.

This is a lithograph of President Chester A. Arthur, who signed the Chinese Exclusion Act into law.

believing that a person's parent was an American citizen. These people are known as paper sons or paper daughters. Another class of undocumented immigrants is the so-called in-transit immigrant, a group who gained entry to America through Mexico and Canada. Immigration was not the only thing the government wanted to restrict. The more extreme voices in the Senate proposed to extend the restriction to trade.

A number of ethnically Chinese merchants and business leaders openly criticized these restrictions. Wong Ar Chong, a Chinese American tea merchant from Boston, invoked the Declaration of Independence, emphasizing that America "is a free country" and that any attempt at restricting immigration or trade would be considered "a backward step being taken by the government."

Resistance was ultimately futile. In 1904, the situation took a turn for the worse: Chinese immigrants residing in the United States were denied the right to apply for citizenship. Further, administrators around the country quickly acted in accordance with the new immigration policies. Angel Island Immigration Station in California was completed in 1910 to screen newcomers more thoroughly. Like Ellis Island in New York, Angel Island was designed to process visitors. But unlike Ellis Island, Angel Island served as a detention point for travelers for prolonged interrogations that could last for days. Asian immigrants were often the targets of investigation as immigration officers tried to expose paper sons and paper daughters.

But it was the Immigration Act of 1924 that marked the peak of Chinese exclusion. The act prohibited all classes of visitors from what was defined as the Asiatic Barred Zone from entering the states. Instead of just barring all classes of Chinese people, the Asiatic Barred Zone prohibited all people from eastern Asia and the Pacific Islands.

VISA UNITED STATE OF AMERIC

A BLESSING IN DISGUISE

The 1906 earthquake in San Francisco was a blessing in disguise for a lot of Chinese immigrants. A fire caused by the earthquake engulfed city hall and the county courthouse and destroyed all the immigration and birth records stored in those buildings. This was a once-in-a-lifetime opportunity for so-called paper sons and paper daughters, because they could claim that their US citizenship documents were lost in the fire. Thus, many undocumented immigrants forged documents about their identities and their family ties to apply for citizenship. Hence, although the law barred Chinese immigrants from becoming American citizens, a group of formerly illegal immigrants obtained legal status that enabled them to work and stay in the United States.

This photograph portrays members of the Chinese community in San Francisco's Chinatown neighborhood after the 1906 earthquake. Note the smoky sky and littered streets.

Anti-Chinese regulation did not only affect newcomers, it also changed the political and cultural climate for Chinese Americans. Persons of Chinese descent were treated like second-class citizens. Hate crimes and police raids targeting ethnic Chinese residents were commonplace. Chinese exclusion also affected immigrants on a deeply personal level: those who had been waiting to reunite with their family members could not bring their families to the United States.

Fighting Chinese Exclusion

The repeal of the Chinese Exclusion Act happened when it was convenient for the US government, although activists and Asian groups had been making persistent demands for it. The government's attitude toward Asia changed drastically only after the Japanese military attacked Pearl Harbor in Hawaii on December 7, 1941.

PROTEST AGAINST ANTI-CHINESE POLICIES

Chinese workers who faced deportation in the United States fought for themselves in court. However, the Naturalization Act of 1906 made the fight more difficult. That act mandated that the government transfer deportation cases to an office called the Bureau of Immigration and Naturalization. This

President Theodore Roosevelt works at his desk in 1906. This was the same year he signed the Naturalization Act of 1906 into law.

office's advent shifted the burden of proof of citizenship to the accused.

The policies of Chinese exclusion not only offended the Imperial Government in China, but it also drew the ire of ordinary Chinese people. According to the writing of Wong Sin-Kiong, an assistant professor and assistant head of the Department of Chinese Studies at the National University of Singapore, as early as 1903, Honolulu-based newspaper *Xin Zhongguo Bao* floated the idea of a boycott. The reason that the paper offered was clear from the article's title: "Proposing the Tactic of Boycotting Exclusion Laws."

Wong also wrote about how the idea of the boycott spread throughout Shanghai in a newspaper called *Shibao* in August 1904. The idea caught on in Hong Kong and throughout mainland China, and the merchants of Shanghai issued a boycott resolution in May 1905. This collective rejection of American goods clearly demonstrated their grievances and put pressure on the US government to lift the anti-Chinese immigration restriction. However, the restriction was not lifted in the end because the United States acknowledged the compelling arguments of Chinese immigrants or Chinese merchants.

REPEALING THE CHINESE EXCLUSION ACT

The United States finally moved away from Chinese exclusion when China and the United States became allies in World War II. When immigration exclusion was first introduced in

FIGHTING ANTI-CHINESE PREJUDICE IN COURT

In the United States, small steps were taken against anti-Chinese prejudice before World War II. For example, *Yick Wo v. Hopkins* (1886) was the result of the owner of a laundry (whose name may or may not have been Yick Wo), suing after he was arrested by Sheriff Peter Hopkins in San Francisco. The laundry did not have the special permit required for laundries operating in wooden buildings in San Francisco. In fact, none of the Chinese laundry owners who applied for the permit was granted one. In contrast, most of the white laundromat owners managed to get permission. Thus, the owner accused Hopkins of enforcing rules in a discriminatory manner.

Wo was initially convicted and fined and then jailed after refusing to pay the fine, but his counsel appealed the conviction all the way to the Supreme Court. The US Supreme Court ultimately reversed Yick Wo's conviction unanimously on the grounds that it was unconstitutional. It was a landmark US Supreme Court case that was later cited in petitions about discriminatory administration and enforcement of laws. It was one small step for Yick Wo, and one giant leap for minorities in America.

1882, Japan was considered a favored nation and was therefore excluded from the Asiatic Barred Zone. Unlike the Chinese, Japanese visitors were given relatively free entry to America. However, as xenophobic sentiments grew stronger, the privilege once conferred to the Japanese was stripped away.

Things went from bad to worse for Japanese people and Japanese Americans in the United States after the United States declared war on Japan on December 8, 1941. People of Japanese descent in America were subject to varying degrees of mistreatment. Further, the main target of discrimination shifted from the Chinese to the Japanese as the US government pondered questions of Japanese loyalty.

Since both the United States and China were committed to defeating Japan, Sino-American relations warmed up. In order to form alliances with China in the Pacific region, Washington felt compelled to soften its stance against the Chinese government and Chinese immigrants. President Franklin D. Roosevelt tried to urge Americans to change their attitudes toward immigrants from China. In a speech Roosevelt made while conducting his southern tour, he said, "We cannot expect China to do us justice unless we do China justice." He meant to highlight the importance of granting entry to all Chinese. A repeal appeared to be inevitable.

In 1943, it finally happened. Congress passed the Magnuson Act, also known as the Chinese Exclusion Repeal Act. The US Department of State admitted that the repeal of the Chinese Exclusion Act was "almost wholly grounded in the exigencies of World War II." The federal government likely feared that the enforcement of the Chinese Exclusion Act would weaken ties

US Representative Warren G. Magnuson proposed the Magnuson Act. The act allowed the Chinese to enter the United States, but it continued the ban on Chinese people owning property and businesses.

between the two countries and undermine the war effort. It served as a grand diplomatic gesture that perhaps meant to try to paper over historic wrongs. In any case, the passage of the Magnuson Act was monumental as it officially put an end to the era of Chinese exclusion. Chinese residents in the United States could become naturalized again. However, prejudices against the Chinese community remained.

LIMITED ENTRY

Immigration restriction did not end entirely with the Magnuson Act. An immigration quota was introduced in 1943, and it limited Chinese immigration to 105 people per year. This number is extremely small in light of the tens of thousands of Chinese laborers who came to the United States each year from the 1850s to the 1870s. A small number of undocumented immigrants risked deportation to come to America, but in general, Chinese immigration remained low during this time.

However, not all doors were closed. Nonquota entry permits were granted for immigrants under special circumstances. One example of a nonquota immigrant is the war bride. The Alien Fiancées and Fiancés Act of 1946, coupled with the 1947 amendment to the War Brides Act, allowed Chinese American servicemen to bring their wives to America. Gary Okihiro writes in *American History Unbound: Asians and Pacific Islanders* that 12,041 Chinese Americans served during World War II. Of those, many of them were

War brings chaos, but it also brings chances for upward mobility. World War II opened up new opportunities for Chinese Americans in particular. In the late nineteenth and early twentieth centuries, most Chinese Americans were stuck with jobs in Chinatown because they were not desirable in the mainstream job market. These jobs did not pay well, so Chinese immigrants had no choice but to dwell at the bottom of the economic ladder and to live on the margins of society. In comparison, Chinese American

So Tai Wong and Elizabeth CNG serve newly inducted service members at a church in New York City's Chinatown.

servicemen received better pay and benefits. Those who served in the war were also granted scholarships for college education, thanks to the Montgomery GI Bill. In total, 12,041 Chinese Americans served in World War II. Their participation in the war changed the socioeconomic status of their community.

For Chinese Americans, serving in the military also had a deeper meaning. It was proof that the American dream was still alive. It validated that every American, regardless of race or origin, could improve his social station as long as he was willing to work hard; it meant that they were finally given an equal opportunity. The uniforms these servicemen donned made them feel more American than ever before.

dispatched to China. Under the 1945 War Brides Act and the Alien Fiancées and Fiancés Act of 1946, one hundred thousand spouses of soldiers and veterans—not exclusively Chinese American—came to the United States. These regulations drastically changed the gender ratio of Chinese Americans. Previously, the majority of Chinese immigrants were male laborers; now, young women featured more prominently in the statistics.

The immigration quota for the Chinese was finally lifted in 1965, when Congress passed the amendment to the 1952 Immigration and Nationality Act. The Immigration

These Chinese war brides, who moved to the United States during and after World War II, attend Sunday school in 1950 in an effort to assimilate into American culture.

and Nationality Act of 1965, an amendment also known as the Hart-Celler Act, set the same visa quota for all countries and was meant to ensure fairness to all newcomers. After that, the United States saw a surge in Chinese immigration.

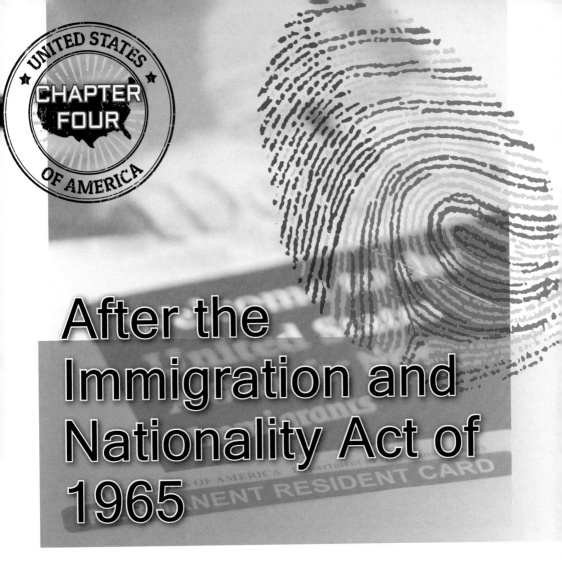

After the Immigration and Nationality Act of 1965

The immigration quota was lifted in 1968 under the Immigration and Nationality Act of 1965. A range of options opened up to ethnic Chinese people from mainland China, Hong Kong, Macau, and Taiwan. Some came on student or work visas. Some applied to set up businesses. Others signed up for immigrant investor programs. Those who wanted to flee the communist regime that came to power often viewed America as the ideal destination as well.

Still, there were some who were excluded from legal entry. Those who did not meet the requirements in the immigration categories did not necessarily give up. If they could pay, snake-heads, or smugglers, would bring them to the United States.

A NEW WAVE OF IMMIGRANTS

After the Immigration and Nationality Act of 1965, the US government firmly stood by the belief that China, Hong Kong, and Taiwan were three different states that would receive equal treatment. Thus, the three jurisdictions were granted the same visa quota. Naturally, the number of immigrants from China was relatively small. Combined, Chinese immigration grew in the 1970s, but very slowly.

Chinese immigrants who arrived from China after 1965 were more diverse than those in the first wave. Compared to the earlier generations of immigrants, the new group was made up of more professionals, business owners, and schol-ars. The United States, a country that highly values rights and freedoms (even if they are not in practice always given to all), is also a top choice for Chinese citizens who fear per-secution and need protection from another government. In particular, the Cultural Revolution, which began in 1966, turned many capitalists and intellectuals into refugees. Those who were oppressed under the regime felt the need to flee their homeland, and a significant number of them migrated to the United States.

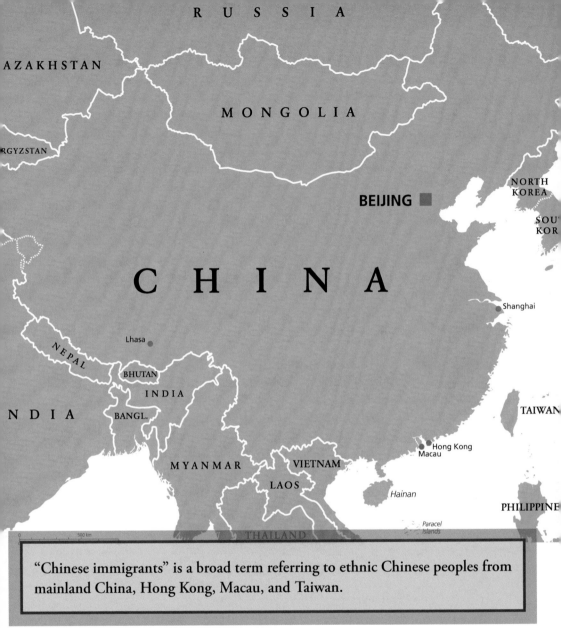

RUSSIA

KAZAKHSTAN

MONGOLIA

RGYZSTAN

BEIJING

NORTH
KOREA

SOU'
KOR

C H I N A

Shanghai

NEPAL

Lhasa

BHUTAN

INDIA

NDIA

BANGL.

TAIWAN

Hong Kong
Macau

MYANMAR

VIETNAM

LAOS

Hainan

PHILIPPINE

Paracel
Islands

500 km

THAILAND

"Chinese immigrants" is a broad term referring to ethnic Chinese peoples from
mainland China, Hong Kong, Macau, and Taiwan.

Chinese Americans are now no longer the homogeneous image of impoverished laborers and laundry owners. Chinese Americans today are more educated and wealthier than they have ever been. As of 2015, US Census data shows that 53.9 percent of Asians in the United States (citizens and permanent residents) above the age of twenty-five have a bachelor's degree—an astonishing achievement given that only 32.5 percent of Americans overall achieved the same level of education. According to Pew Research Center analysis extrapolated from the 2010 US Census, the median annual household income of Chinese Americans is $65,050, a figure that is about $15,000 higher than average earnings in the United States ($49,800).

While this shift in economic status was occurring, the United States saw a greater increase in Chinese immigration in the 1980s as its relations with the government of China improved. In 1980, 812,178 Chinese immigrants arrived in the United States. That number grew to 1,645,472 in 1990, according to US Census data from 1990, and 2,858,291 in 2000's US Census. It was between these years that the Chinese immigrant population grew the fastest. By 2010, the number of Chinese Americans reached 3.3 to 4 million ethnic Chinese, with figures being smaller for those who identified as being exclusively Chinese and rising for mixed-race individuals who had some Chinese heritage, according to the 2010 US census.

Another type of immigration also became available to the Chinese at this time. As China's economy picked up, an increasing number of Chinese immigrants are opting for a different immigration visa category: an investment program. Under the current immigration laws, foreigners who are capable of investing in the United States to create jobs can be granted green cards. The US government created the EB-5 investor program in 1990 to attract foreign investors. Invest in the USA, an EB-5 trade association, compiled federal data and found that 85 percent of the ten thousand

EB-5 visas that are issued each year go to Chinese nationals. For the wealthy, it is a lucrative way to gain passage to the United States through legal means.

However, immigration programs do not capture the whole picture of Chinese immigration after the Immigration and Naturalization Act of 1965. Unauthorized immigration is an important, but often overlooked, aspect of Chinese immigration history. According to a March 2017 article from the *New York Times*, there were an estimated 268,000 undocumented immigrants from China. Complicating unauthorized status is the fact that China doesn't cooperate with the United States in deportation activities.

AN EVOLVING LANDSCAPE

New stereotypes about Chinese people have emerged as they have achieved new heights. Chinese Americans are often characterized as overachieving and hypercompetitive. This stereotype is epitomized in Amy Chua's 2011 memoir *The Battle Hymn of the Tiger Mother*, an autobiographical account of a Chinese American mom who used strict discipline methods to help her daughters achieve academic success. Reactions from Chinese Americans to the TV series *Fresh off the Boat*, a comedy about a Chinese American family, suggest that there may be some truth in this stereotype, while other reactions on the *Huffington Post*, *The Mary Sue*, and *Time* magazine widely condemned or applauded the show overall for its depiction of a Taiwanese American family.

145B

SHUN 儁 面 貨 VARIETY STORE

This photo shows the storefront that Cheng Chui Ping claimed was her main business. It is located in New York City's Chinatown.

Since the passage of the Immigration and Nationality Act of 1965, most undocumented immigrants have relied on human smugglers to reach the United States. Cheng Chui Ping, in particular, was revered and feared by those who wished to cross the seas and attain the American dream. Nicknamed Big Sister Ping, her smuggling business was worth roughly forty million dollars at its peak.

Too profit driven to care about safety, she was not afraid to

VISA

UNITED STAT

use faulty ships to bring undocumented immigrants from China to America. In 1993, she notoriously packed three hundred migrants in an old freighter that ran aground. Ten people died. Ping also allegedly hired gangs to threaten family members of immigrants who had failed to pay their debts.

She was arrested in 2000 and received a thirty-five year prison sentence.

While Chinese Americans have made incredible progress in closing education and wage gaps with white Americans, the fight against stereotypes and new problems remains to be won. For starters, distrust of Chinese immigrants remains. One of the reasons for distrust is the suspicion that Chinese Americans may be working for foreign powers. Wen Ho Lee, a Taiwan-born scientist, was investigated and arrested by the Federal Bureau of Investigation (FBI) in 1999 for leaking nuclear secrets to China. This incident was a particularly high-profile case of Chinese espionage. He was imprisoned for nine months under false pretenses that the US government concocted in an egregious abuse of power, but he ultimately agreed to a plea deal that didn't implicate him in sharing secrets with China. Afterward, he wasn't able to find a teaching job, and the investigation cost him his former job working for the University of California at the Los Alamos National Laboratory.

Lee was not the only one who faced such unfounded accusations. Over the years, there have been many similar

investigations concerning alleged Chinese spies. In 2015, Dr. George Koo, a former adviser at a global advisory services firm, wrote an opinion piece for the *Asia Times* called "Chinese Americans Continue to Be Victimized by Racial Profiling" that detailed several cases of racial profiling. He discusses the struggle of Sherry Chen to be freed after being accused of espionage in 2014 and the struggle of Dr. Bo Jiang, a subcontractor for the National Aeronautics and Space Administration (NASA) who planned to return to China after his contract ended. The US government scrutinized these individuals in spite of little evidence supporting claims of espionage. Their charges were made simply on the assumption that acts like leaving the United States for China and meeting with a former classmate who now holds a high position in China's government indicated intent to commit espionage. The charges for these two individuals were dropped, but there have been more substantial charges that remained for Chinese people accused on much stronger evidence. Regardless, it seems likely that America's suspicion of Chinese espionage will remain an enduring obstacle for Chinese Americans in their pursuit of acceptance.

INCREASED PARTICIPATION IN BUSINESS, POLITICS, AND THE MEDIA

Chinese American representation in different sectors and industries, including politics, business, art, entertainment, and

academia, is increasing steadily. In particular, more and more Chinese Americans are found in industries that are not traditionally associated with the Chinese identity.

Elaine L. Chao served as deputy director of transportation and director of the Peace Corps under President George H. W. Bush. She served as secretary of labor under President George W. Bush. After holding these positions, she served in several other capacities, including as the secretary of transportation in President Donald Trump's administration. These appointments contradicted the idea that Chinese Americans are absent or invisible in domestic American politics. Ali Wong, a stand-up comedian and television writer, is successful despite an overall lack of Asian women in the comedy scene. Wong used comedy as a platform to provide groundbreaking and incisive comments about the experience of being a minority in the United States. And Steven Chen, cofounder of YouTube, contradicts the stereotype that Chinese Americans are not particularly creative or adventurous. Individuals like these contribute to a more nuanced image of Chinese people by reshaping the narrative. They are no longer seen as the exotic foreigners who bring new vices to America; instead, they have generally proven themselves to be industrious, upstanding members of society.

However, this is not to say that Chinese Americans do not face challenges in their professional lives anymore. According to Ascend, a New York-based Asian American professional organization, Asian Americans have a hard time getting promoted in technology-related work. The situation is worse for women: on average, only 1 in 285 working Asian women is an executive, which is much lower than the national average

Elaine L. Chao was confirmed as the secretary of transportation on January 31, 2017.

VISA UNITED STATES OF AMERICA

(1 executive per 118 professionals). This statistic suggests that there are few Asian American leaders despite the high employment rate in the community. This discrepancy may have to do with Asian or Chinese American stereotypes or culture, both of which may expect Asian Americans to be less outspoken and thus less likely to be seen as leaders.

MOVING TO SUBURBS AND INNER CITIES

As the socioeconomic status of Chinese Americans improved during the postwar era, their lifestyles also changed. In the past, most of them lived in Chinatowns in New York, San Francisco, and other cities. However, this is no longer a given. In 2015, *New York* magazine published an article called "How Has Chinatown Stayed Chinatown?" in which Nick Tabor explores how Chinese Americans and immigrants managed to gain control of New York City's Chinatown neighborhood by buying land and setting rules that accommodate their ability to afford living and doing business there. Tabor explored how while buying land is a strategy that maintains control, the question of where later generations choose to live also has an impact on the demographics of the neighborhood. The situation was much more grim in Washington, DC, in 2015, the year that a *Washington Post* article announced in its title that "D.C.'s Chinatown Has Only 300 Chinese Americans Left, and They're Fighting to Stay."

Leaving Chinatowns may have a positive impact on Chinese Americans. Leaving often results in Chinese Americans

VESTIGE OF DISCRIMINATION

Despite the achievements of the Chinese American community, hate crimes still remain a huge concern for Chinese Americans. The story of Vincent Chin is one case in particular that gained a lot of attention from the media in 1982.

The rise of Japanese cars began to impact the US manufacturing industry by the 1980s. That is why two white men in a Detroit bar clubbed Chin to death after mistaking him for a Japanese man. Before Chin died, his killers yelled expletives, blaming him for putting them out of work. He was twenty-seven years old.

What transpired that day is reminiscent of the anti-Chinese massacre of the nineteenth century. And other than the egregious brutality of it, the story also demonstrates that to some Americans, all Asians are the same. Furthermore, the case highlights that some white Americans still hold the belief that they are more American than Chinese Americans or other Asian Americans. As such, they feel entitled to the achievements of Chinese Americans. It is likely that the rise of China as a world power and the recession of American power will cause anti-Chinese sentiments to linger in the United States.

Outside of violence, many Chinese Americans deal with prejudice on a daily basis. Michael Luo, a reporter for the *New York Times* in 2016, wrote about when in that year he was told by a pedestrian that he should "go back to China" and "go back to [his]... country." Recounting the experience, Luo wrote about "this persistent sense of otherness that a lot of [Chinese Americans] struggle with every day." It is clear that some still insist on seeing Chinese Americans as an exotic, incomprehensible other that cannot be accepted as one of us.

Vincent Chin was murdered by white men who resented the emergence of Japanese competition in car manufacturing.

The Chinatown in downtown Manhattan is still thriving after approximately one hundred years. These protruding signboards are reminiscent of the streets in Hong Kong.

becoming more integrated. Initially, white Americans might have resisted the notion of Chinese immigrants and Chinese Americans relocating to the suburbs, but over time, their presence outside Chinatown helps bridge the gap between Americans and new immigrants. Chinatown was created as a result of marginalization, but the demographic shift that is happening to Chinatown is a sign of displacement or assimilation.

WHERE CHINESE AMERICANS STAND

Adaptation and assimilation are nebulous concepts that come with subjective experiences. There are quantitative and qualitative measures of success that usually illustrate how well immigrants have assimilated into the United States by looking at how similar they are to typical Americans in terms of their socioeconomic status, education level, civic mindedness, and lifestyles.

Despite the gains that were previously outlined, many Chinese Americans still report feeling isolated. According to the Pew Research Center, more than half of them see themselves as very different from the typical American. In fact, in everyday life, only 14 percent tend to describe themselves as American (as opposed to Asian American, Chinese American, or Chinese). A more telling sign is their social circles: among Asian Americans, immigrants and American-born included, about 40 percent claim that most of their friends are ethnically Chinese. Among US-born Asians, only 17 percent make that claim.

MYTHS AND FACTS

MYTH

Chinese people eat dogs.

FACT

Although Western media is preoccupied with China's Dog Meat Festival, only a minority of Chinese people eats dog meat. It is safe to say that dog eating is being phased out, especially in the Chinese American community. Even in China, most people do not eat dog meat because the younger generation tends to view dogs as pets and part of the family.

MYTH

Chinese people are naturally good at math.

FACT

The assertion that Chinese people are good at math is a running joke in television shows and films. There is an abundance of anecdotal evidence of Chinese students excelling at math, but there is no body of evidence that examines the matter of whether the Chinese have an inherent advantage in the subject. The Confucian work ethic may be behind the motivation for Chinese students to apply themselves, or China's educational decision to expose younger students to math that Americans don't encounter until high school may give students from China an advantage. However, neither of these circumstances indicate a natural ability—they are the result of social conditioning.

MYTH

Chinese people were the ones who brought the laundry business to America.

FACT

Many early Chinese immigrants chose to run laundromats and dry cleaners because of the low barrier to entry in the market. Immigrants turned this low-skill work into a business when few other jobs were open to them.

Laundering is not a traditional trade in China. There were no laundry businesses in China during the nineteenth century. In fact, most women did the laundry for their families in the tub or by a stream.

FACT SHEET

CHINESE AMERICANS

Population

Chinese Americans are one of the fastest-growing groups of minorities in the United States. As of 2017, there were approximately 3.8 million Chinese Americans. They live predominantly on the West Coast and in the Northeast. There is also a large ethnically Chinese population in Hawaii.

Major Holidays

Chinese people observe an array of holidays and customs.

- The Lunar New Year and the Mid-Autumn festivals are two major holidays for the Chinese. The Lunar New Year festival, in particular, is a fifteen-day-long celebration that involves spring cleaning, decorating, shopping, family reunions, and sharing food. It is also many Chinese children's favorite holiday because children and young single adults typically receive red packets, red envelopes that contain money.
- Mid-Autumn Festival celebrates the end of the autumn harvest. It is also known as Moon Festival because it is celebrated on the full moon.
- There is no major Chinese religious holiday. In fact, about half of Chinese immigrants claim that they are not affiliated with any religion. The other half is mainly a mix of Buddhists, Protestants, Catholics, and Taoists.

60

VISA UNITED STATE

Major Foods

Chinese immigrants are also known for their ethnic cuisine. "Chinese food," however, is an umbrella term that does not capture the complexity and diversity of cuisines from the different parts of China. Most of the dishes on a typical Chinese food menu in American restaurants have roots in Cantonese, Taishanese, or Fujianese recipes. These three regions are where early immigrants came from. As more immigrants from other parts of China have come to the United States, the repertoire of Chinese food has expanded.

Languages Spoken

- A significant number of Chinese Americans are bilingual. More than half of Chinese immigrants are fluent in English. At the same time, about 44 percent of those born in the United States can converse in their native language.
- Native language does not necessarily mean Mandarin. Mandarin is the official language in China and Taiwan, but dialects including Cantonese, Taishanese, and Hokkien are more widely spoken in southern China, where many Chinese immigrants came from.

TIMELINE

1848 Individual Chinese immigrants start coming to America, and the first Chinatown is established in San Francisco.

1849 Chinese laborers arrive to join the California gold rush.

1850 The Taiping Rebellion breaks out in China. This event serves as the primary motivating factor for more Chinese people to emigrate.

1862 The California government mandates that every Chinese person age eighteen or over must pay a police tax of $2.50 per month.

1863 Workers begin constructing the Transcontinental Railroad. After this, more and more Chinese laborers sign up to work for railroad companies despite the unequal pay between white and nonwhite workers.

1871 An anti-Chinese riot takes place in Los Angeles. Seventeen Chinese immigrants—men and boys—are killed.

1872 The Qing government in China sponsors thirty male students to study in the United States. This marks the first time Chinese scholars arrived in America.

1882 President Chester A. Arthur signs the Chinese Exclusion Act to impose immigration restrictions on Chinese laborers.

1885 On February 7, three hundred Chinese immigrants are banished from Eureka, California after a violent confrontation.

On September 2, a clash between white and Chinese coal miners in Rock Springs, Wyoming takes place. It takes the lives of twenty-eight Chinese laborers.

1906 On April 18, an earthquake hits San Francisco. It causes a fire in municipal buildings that destroys immigration records. Following this incident, many undocumented immigrants make fraudulent claims of citizenship.

1910 Angel Island Immigration Station in California is completed. Its purpose is to allow immigration officers to detain and interrogate new immigrants, especially those from Asia.

1924 The Immigration Act of 1924 prohibits all Chinese people from entering the United States.

1943 Congress passes the Magnuson Act, also known as the Chinese Exclusion Repeal Act. A quota is established: 105 Chinese immigrants are allowed per year.

1947 The 1947 amendment to the War Brides Act, along with the 1946 Alien Fiancées and Fiancés Act, enables those who married American servicemen to come to the United States on a nonquota basis.

1965 The Immigration and Nationality Act of 1965 is passed.

1990 The US government creates the EB-5 investor program.

2017 Approximately 3.8 million Chinese people (immigrants or naturalized citizens) live in the United States.

assimilation The process by which an individual or a group becomes more like another group in its socioeconomic status, educational level, psychological state, and culture.

barrier to entry The level of difficulty in starting up a new business.

Chinatown A neighborhood in certain large cities that has a high concentration of Chinese residents and workers.

compatriots One's countrymen or countrywomen; people from the same country.

credit-ticket system A recruitment system under which employers would pay for a migrant workers' travel, and workers would pay their employees back with their labor.

emigrant An expatriate; one who leaves his or her native country for another land.

enclave A surrounded place with a distinct culture or people.

first-generation An adjective that describes a person who is the first generation of the family to achieve a specific feat, like first-generation college students.

gateway city A port city where immigrants first landed and settled. For Chinese immigrants, gateway cities include San Francisco, Los Angeles, and New York City.

immigrant A permanent expatriate; one who has decided to settle forever in a country other than the one where they are from.

inadvertently Unintentionally; not on purpose.

mass migration A reactionary phenomenon in which people leave one geographical area for another due to some hardship that threatens their survival.

minority A racial, ethnic, sexual, or some other type or group of people that does not make up the group with the greatest number of people in a place.

misconception A false assumption or belief.

otherness The quality of being radically different and therefore incomprehensible.

Pacific theater The region in and around the Pacific Ocean where World War II was fought.

paper sons/daughters Unauthorized Chinese immigrants who gained entry into the United States by forging familial ties.

queue A men's hairstyle that denoted loyalty to the Qing dynasty. Hair at the top of the head would be cut off. Hair in the back would be grown long and braided.

semicolonial state A country that has lost some of its control over trade and economy to a foreign power but still maintains its courts.

Sino- An adjectival prefix that means "Chinese." Used in the context of Sino-American, or Sino- (country's demonym) to denote international relations between China and that country.

xenophobia Fear of a different country's nationals.

FOR MORE INFORMATION

Asia Society
725 Park Avenue
New York, NY 10021
(212) 288-6400
Website: http://asiasociety.org
Facebook: @asiasociety
Twitter: @asiasociety
Asia Society is a nonprofit organization that aims to promote bicultural understanding in Asia and the United States. The Center for Global Education at Asia Society provides free resources on the history as well as demographic data about Asian Americans.

Center for Chinese Studies (CCS) at University of Hawaii at Manoa
Moore Hall 417
1890 East-West Road
Honolulu, HI 96822
(808) 956-8891
Website: http://www.ccs-uhm.org
CCS at the University of Hawaii stays in the forefront of research in Chinese culture and Chinese American immigrant history. It offers free resources and runs trainings courses on Chinese culture and international studies.

Chinese American Museum, Los Angeles
425 North Los Angeles Street
Los Angeles, CA 90012
(213) 485-8567

Website: http://camla.org
Facebook: @chineseamericanmuseum
Instagram: @camlaorg
Twitter: @camlaorg
Located in the old Chinatown of Los Angeles, the Chinese
    American Museum showcases artifacts that carry stories
    about Chinese immigrants.

Chinese Canadian Stories
2329 West Mall
Vancouver, BC V6T 1Z4
Canada
(604) 827-4366
Website: http://chinesecanadian.ubc.ca
Facebook: @chinesecanadian
Twitter: @chinesecanadian
YouTube: @chinesecanadianubc
Chinese Canadian Stories is an initiative that helps Chinese
    immigrants in Canada document their family histories. As
    such, this project has digitized research tools and materials
    for scholars who are interested in Chinese studies.

Chinese Cultural Center Museum and Archive (Vancouver)
106 Keefer Street
Vancouver, BC V6A 1X4
Canada
(604) 632-3808
Website: http://www.vancouver-chinatown.com/attractions
    /sceneries.php

Exhibits at Vancouver's Chinese Cultural Center tell stories about the earliest Chinese immigrants in Canada. The center also hosts education programs and walking tours to promote Chinese arts and culture.

Pew Research Center
1615 L Street NW, Suite 800
Washington, DC 20036
(202) 419-4300
Website: http://www.pewresearch.org
Facebook: @pewresearch
Twitter: @pewresearch
The Pew Research Center has published thorough studies on Asian Americans, including Chinese Americans. Its research not only looks at the socioeconomic status of Chinese Americans, but also pays attention to the way Chinese Americans feel about their conditions.

Smithsonian Asian Pacific American Center
Capital Gallery, Suite 7065
600 Maryland Avenue SW
Washington, DC 20024
(202) 633-2691
Website: http://smithsonianapa.org
Facebook: @SmithsonianAPA
Instagram: @SmithsonianAPA
Twitter: @SmithsonianAPA
The Smithsonian Asian Pacific American Center is an online project that promotes Asian Pacific American arts and

cultures. It relies on a variety of digital platforms to revolutionize the museum-going experience.

US Census Bureau
4600 Silver Hill Road
Washington, DC 20233
(800) 923-8282
Website: https://www.census.gov/programs-surveys/acs
Twitter: @uscensusbureau
The American Community Survey is commissioned by the
     US Census Bureau to mine information about the shifting
     demographics in the United States. It regularly releases
     reports on new trends in the Asian American community.

FOR FURTHER READING

Chang, Gordon H. *Fateful Ties: A History of America's Preoccupation with China.* Cambridge, MA: Harvard University Press, 2015.

Huang, Eddie. *Fresh off the Boat: A Memoir.* New York, NY: Spiegel & Grau, 2013.

Huang, Yunte. *The Big Red Book of Modern Chinese Literature: Writings from the Mainland in the Long Twentieth Century.* New York, NY: W. W. Norton & Company, 2016.

Hui Wang, Hui. *Chin's Twentieth Century.* London, UK: Verso, 2016.

Mao, Haijian. *The Qing Empire and the Opium War: The Collapse of the Heavenly Dynasty.* New York, NY: Cambridge University Press, 2016.

Seligman, Scott D. *Three Tough Chinamen.* Hong Kong: Earnshaw Books, 2012.

Shang, Wendy. *The Great Wall of Lucy Wu.* New York, NY: Scholastic, 2013.

Wasserstrom, Jeffrey N. *The Oxford Illustrated History of Modern China.* New York, NY: Oxford University Press, 2016.

Widmer, Ellen. *Fiction's Family: Zhan Xi, Zhan Kai, and the Business of Women in Late-Qing China.* Cambridge, MA: Harvard University Asia Center, 2016.

Yang, Binbin. *Heroines of the Qing.* Seattle, WA: University of Washington Press, 2016.

Aoki, Keith. "No Right to Own? The Early Twentieth-Century 'Alien Land Laws' as a Prelude to Internment." *Boston College Third World Law Journal.* Vol. 19, Issue 1. 1998.

Ascend Foundation. "Hidden in Plain Sight: Asian American Leaders in Silicon Valley." May 2015. http://c.ymcdn .com/sites/ascendleadership.site-ym.com/resource/resmgr /Research/HiddenInPlainSight_Paper_042.pdf.

Bigelow, Martha, and Johanna Ennser-Kananen. *The Rout-ledge Handbook of Educational Linguistics.* Abingdon, UK: Routledge, 2014.

Center for Labor Education & Research at the University of Hawaiʻi, West Oʻahu. "History of Labor in Hawaiʻi." Retrieved September 8, 2017. https://www.hawaii.edu /uhwo/clear/home/HawaiiLaborHistory.html.

Central Pacific Railroad Photographic History Museum. "Chinese-American Contribution to Transcontinental Railroad." Retrieved September 8, 2017. http://cprr.org /Museum/Chinese.html.

Chan, Sucheng. "The Economic Life of the Chinese in California, 1850–1920." *Early Chinese Immigrant Societies: Case Studies from North America and British Southeast Asia.* Kallang, Singapore: Heinemann Asia, 1988.

Chong, Wong Ar. Letter to William Lloyd Garrison. February 28, 1879. Republished in Slate on May 28, 2014.

Chua, Amy. *The Battle Hymn of the Tiger Mother.* New York, NY: Penguin, 2011.

Curran, Enda, Jun Luo, Dingmin Zhang, and Caleb Melby. "Rich Chinese Race to Apply for a U.S. Golden Visa."

Bloomberg News, March 26, 2017. https://www .bloomberg.com/news/articles/2017-03-26/rich-chinese -race-to-fund-kushner-tower-other-high-end-projects.

Fish, Eric. "35 Years After Vincent Chin's Murder, How Has America Changed?" Asia Society, June 16, 2017. http:// asiasociety.org/blog/asia/35-years-after-vincent-chins -murder-how-has-america-changed.

Foster, John W. "The Chinese Boycott." *The Atlantic Monthly*, Volume 97. Cambridge, MA: The Riverside Press, 1906.

Gompers, Samuel, and Herman Gutstadt. "Some Reasons for Chinese Exclusion. Meat vs. Rice. American Manhood Against Asiatic Coolieism. Which Shall Survive?" Columbus, OH: American Federation of Labor, 1902.

Hong, Jane H. "The Repeal of Asian Exclusion." *Oxford Research Encyclopedias*, September 2015. http:// americanhistory.oxfordre.com/view/10.1093/acrefore /9780199329175.001.0001/acrefore-9780199329175 -e-16.

Koo, George. "Chinese Americans Continue to Be Victimized by Racial Profiling." *Asia Times*, May 18, 2015. http:// www.atimes.com/article/chinese-americans-continue-to -be-victimized-by-racial-profiling-opinion.

Lee, Erika. *The Making of Asian America: A History.* New York, NY: Simon & Schuster, 2015.

Luo, Michael. "An Open Letter to the Woman Who Told My Family to Go Back to China." *New York Times*, Oct 9, 2016. https://www.nytimes.com/2016/10/10/nyregion /to-the-woman-who-told-my-family-to-go-back-to-china .html.

McCunn, Ruthanne Lum. *An Illustrated History of the Chinese in America.* San Francisco, CA: Design Enterprises of San Francisco, 1979.

Migration Policy Institute. "Chinese Americans in the United States." January 28, 2015. http://www.migrationpolicy .org/article/chinese-immigrants-united-states.

Onion, Rebecca. "A Chinese-American Merchant's Blistering Arguments Against Chinese Exclusion." *Slate*, May 28, 2014. http://www.slate.com/blogs/the_vault/2014/05/28 /chinese_exclusion_act_letter_from_chinese_american _merchant_to_william_lloyd.html.

PBS. "Documents on Anti-Chinese Immigration Policy." New Perspectives on the West. Retrieved September 8, 2017. http://www.pbs.org/weta/thewest/resources/archives /seven/chinxact.htm.

PBS. "The Story of Chinatown." Chinatown Resource Guide. Retrieved September 7, 2017. http://www.pbs.org/kqed /chinatown/resourceguide/story.html.

Pew Research Center. *The Rise of Asian Americans.* April 4, 2013. http://www.pewsocialtrends.org/asianamericans -graphics/chinese.

Samuel, Deborah. "Chinese Immigration, Exclusion and the Chinese American Experience." Yale National Initiative. Retrieved July 20, 2017. http://teachers.yale.edu /curriculum/viewer/initiative_06.02.06_u.

Smithsonian National Museum of American History. "Liners to America." Retrieved August 1, 2017. http:// americanhistory.si.edu/onthewater/exhibition/5_2.html.

Stahl, Jessica. "What Was It Like to Be a Chinese Student in 19th Century America?" VOA News, August 16, 2012. https://blogs.voanews.com/student-union/2012/08/16 /what-was-it-like-to-be-a-chinese-student-in-19th-century -america.

Tabor, Nick. "How Has Chinatown Stayed Chinatown?" New York, September 24, 2015. http://nymag.com/daily /intelligencer/2015/09/how-has-chinatown-stayed -chinatown.html.

Tsai, Shih-Shan Henry. *The Chinese Experience in America.* Bloomington, IN: Indiana University Press, 1986.

Tsui, Bonnie. *American Chinatown: A People's History of Five Neighborhoods.* New York, NY: Free Press, 2010.

US Department of State. "Repeal of the Chinese Exclusion Act, 1943." Retrieved September 11, 2017. https:// history.state.gov/milestones/1937-1945/chinese-exclusion -act-repeal.

Wang, Yanan. "D.C.'s Chinatown Has Only 300 Chinese Americans Left, and They're Fighting to Stay." Washington Post, July 18, 2015. https://www.washingtonpost. com/lifestyle/style/dcs-chinatown-has-only-300-chinese -americans-left--and-fighting-to-stay/2015/07/16 /86d54e84-2191-11e5-bf41-c23f5d3face1_story.html.

Wong, Sin-Kiong. "Mobilizing a Social Movement in China: Propaganda of the 1905 Boycott Campaign." National University of Singapore, 2000. ccs.ncl.edu.tw/Chinese _studies_19_1/375-408.pdf.

Yang, Tim. "The Malleable Yet Undying Nature of the Yellow Peril." Dartmouth College. http://www.dartmouth

.edu/~hist32/History/S22%20-The%20Malleable%20 Yet%20Undying%20Nature%20of%20the%20 Yellow%20Peril.htm.

Zhang, Junmian. "Top 10 Overseas Study Waves in Chinese History." China.org.cn, December 24, 2011. http://www .china.org.cn/top10/2011-12/24/content_24220658 .html.

Zhao, Xiaojian. *Asian American Chronology: Chronologies of the American Mosaic.* Santa Barbara, CA: Greenwood Press, 2009.

Zhao, Xiaojian. *Remaking Chinese America: Immigration, Family, and Community, 1940–1965.* New Brunswick, NJ: Rutgers University Press, 2002.

INDEX

Wasp, The, 28
women's roles, 12, 41, 51
Wong, Ali, 51
Wong Chin Foo, 14–15
Wong Sin-Kiong, 35
World War II, 9, 35–37,
     39–41

X
xenophobia, 23, 37, 37

Y
Yick Wo v. Hopkins, 36

ABOUT THE AUTHOR

Georgina W. S. Lu is an author and scholar who specializes in postcolonialism and cultural studies. She has also studied multilingual poetry and critical theory. Lu is currently a PhD student in the English department of the University of Wisconsin-Madison. Besides her academic pursuits, Lu regularly writes and publishes articles about current affairs, popular culture, and social issues in China. Lu finds this resource on Chinese American history to be deeply personal and meaningful because she comes from a bicultural background.

PHOTO CREDITS

Cover, p. 3 Roberto Soncin Gerometta/Lonely Planet Images/Getty Images; pp. 6–7 FPG/Archive Photos/Getty Images; p. 12 Private Collection/Bridgeman Images; p. 14 Special Collections/University Archives, Bertrand Library, Bucknell University, Lewisburg, Pa.; p. 17 Private Collection/Peter Newark American Pictures/Bridgeman Images; pp. 20, 29, 31, 34 Library of Congress Prints and Photographs Division; p. 24 Fotosearch/Archive Photos/Getty Images; p. 26 © North Wind Picture Archives; p. 38 Ralph Morse/The LIFE Picture Collection/Getty Images; p. 40 © AP Images; p. 42 © Minnesota Historical Society/Corbis Historical/Getty Images; p. 45 Peter Hermes Furian/Shutterstock.com; p. 48 New York Daily News Archive/Getty Images; p. 52 United States Department of Transportation; p. 55 Handout/MCT/Newscom; p. 56 Sean Pavone/Shutterstock.com; cover and back cover (flag) Allies Interactive/Shutterstock.com, (banner) somesh09/Shutterstock.com; interior pages designs (portrait collage) Ollyy/Shutterstock.com, (USA stamp) ducu59us/Shutterstock.com, (fingerprint) Rigamondis/Shutterstock.com, (brochure) Konstanin L/Shutterstock.com, (visa) Sergiy Palamarchuk/Shutterstock.com.

Design: Nelson Sá; Layout: Nicole Russo-Duca;
Editor: Bernadette Davis; Photo Researcher: Nicole DiMella